The Wisdom to Listen

Michael Mitton

Deputy Director of the Acorn Christian Foundation

GROVE BOOKS LIMITED
RIDLEY HALL RD CAMBRIDGE CB3 9HU

Contents

A wise old owl sat on an oak
The more he saw the less he spoke;
The less he spoke the more he heard;
Why aren't we like that wise old bird?
Edward Hersey Richards

Foreword

I should like to record my thanks to those who have helped me in the writing of this booklet. Particularly I am indebted to Anne Long for introducing me to this subject and whose lecture notes on Listening have provided a basis for Chapter 4. Also my thanks to Phyllida, Barbara and Helen who have helped with the typing, spelling, grammar and other literary encouragements. Also to Peter Ashton for the drawings in Chapter 3.

The Cover Illustration is by David Mitton and Clearwater Film Studios Ltd

First Impression February 1981
Reprinted June 1984, November 1986, August 1990, April 1995, December 2002
ISSN 0144-171X
ISBN 1 85174 039 2

Introduction

'It is the province of knowledge to speak,' wrote Holmes, 'and it is the privilege of wisdom to listen.'[1]

He was expressing his belief that the man who is truly wise will first listen, thus gaining certain knowledge, before he speaks. Holmes considers it a privilege to listen to someone, and also a mark of wisdom. At the very beginning of the book of Proverbs it is made clear that it is the *wise* man who will listen to this teaching (Prov 1.5). In the epistle of James it is the man who is 'quick to hear and slow to speak' (Jas 1.19) who is commended. The cry of Job 'Oh, that I had one to hear me' (Job 31.35) is all the more poignant as he has been surrounded by people who have been willing to talk but who have not had the wisdom to listen to Job's suffering. They have given Job advice, before really *hearing* him.[2] To grow in the work of listening is obviously a priority in any form of Christian ministry. Or *is* it obvious?

To grow in the work of listening is obviously a priority in any form of Christian ministry. Or is it obvious?

A dominant characteristic of our day is that of high activity and rush. There is often the persistent urgency to get things done 'in time,' an urgency with which few of our ancestors were plagued. We are pressurized today by a remarkable rate of change where 'the sum of scientific knowledge is doubling every four years, and a piece of research may be out of date before it can be used or even published.'[3] Because of such changes things have to be done fast, important decisions to be made with increasing frequency, and more time is given to *doing*, and less to *reflecting*. In such an age there are many who are prepared to talk, to get their word in before it is too late; many who wish to protest, to express their opinions; there are many who are prepared to exhort, to condemn, to proclaim, to preach. But there are few who are prepared to 'waste' their valuable time in the quiet and apparently unproductive business of listening. For many, it is *not* obvious that growing in the work of listening is a priority.

We would all agree that we have within us certain faculties for communicating messages, and that these faculties require training. We learn a language and carefully use it, with the aid of bodily gestures and facial expressions, to communicate our message. We have had to learn to select suitable words to convey an accurate message. Hopefully we will always be developing our system of communication and our use of language. But when it comes to listening, many would suppose that it is something that 'just happens.' One does not normally think in terms of *learning* to listen, though allowance is often made that some people are 'good' listeners and others 'bad.' However this is not seen as something learned, but rather as some peculiar quality that is part of the personality. The purpose of this booklet is to show that listening is an important quality that *can* be learned and developed.

Few are prepared to 'waste' their valuable time in the apparently unproductive business of listening

In any relationship the ability to listen accurately is of fundamental importance. Failure to be listened to can be distressing. 'He did not even listen!' is a *cri de coeur* that we hear all too often. Conversely, we know the feelings of help and relief when someone is able to listen to us, even when they are not able to give advice or direction.

It is commonly assumed that speaking is the active, positive element of communication, while listening is the purely receptive and passive element. However, listening, though a silent and retiring activity, is far from being passive. Mother Mary Clare, discussing the subject of listening to God, writes:

> To listen, according to the dictionary, is 'attentively to exercise the sense of hearing.' It is not a passive affair, a space when we do not happen to be doing or saying anything and are, therefore, automatically able to listen. It is a conscious, willed action, requiring alertness and vigilance, by which our whole attention is focussed and controlled. So it is difficult.[4]

Because it is difficult and not simply an intuitive, passive response to noise, it needs working on and practice. We have to learn to exercise attentively this sense of hearing that we have been given so that we do effectively hear what a person is communicating, and they may not necessarily be communicating with the words they are using. They may be saying one thing, but in fact be communicating something quite different. The classic example is of a young couple meeting for the first time. They may be talking about what particular films they like and dislike, but in fact on a deeper, unspoken level they may be communicating about their own feelings for each other. There are certain personal and social rules of censorship that necessitate a superficial conversation initially, but nevertheless through these conversations more basic messages are relayed. Accurate listening will hear some of these messages.

It is indeed fitting that the One who is the Word of God showed in his life that he is the one who so accurately listened to people. He has heard the deeper messages beneath the superficial conversations. So when the rich young man comes to Jesus they have a conversation about the commandments, but Jesus hears the real problem, which is that the young man has developed a love for wealth and it is to this need that Jesus speaks (Lk 18.18-23). There are many other such conversations in the gospels, but one of the most significant is that with the Samaritan woman (John 4). In this conversation we find that Jesus listens carefully in the three areas that we are covering in this booklet: he listens to *God*, he listens to the *individual* and he listens to *society*. Jesus begins by listening to the individual. He 'hears' her unspoken words about her tiredness of life. She is thirsty for the type of water that Jesus has come to give. But he does not listen only to the woman. He is also listening to his Father in heaven. Because he is in close touch with his Father, he is open to receiving prophetic insight into the life of this woman, and as he speaks to her about her life, she recognizes him as a prophet (John 4.19). Jesus listened to the woman and he listened to his father. He was also listening to the society in which this woman lived. He 'listened' to the Samaritan/ Jew conflict. He perhaps also listened to the fact that she came all this way out of Sychar (where she probably lived) and she had come on her own. There was much to suggest that her own people had rejected her as a moral outcast. Such thorough listening means that Jesus was able to speak to her with authority and knowledge, such that she returned to her home saying, 'Come, see a man who told me all I ever did' (John 4.29).

The One who is the Word of God showed in his life that he is the one who so accurately listened to people

The *purpose* of listening in these three areas will vary (for instance, I do not listen to God in order to counsel him), but the *methods* of listening, the process of becoming aware, are essentially the same. Therefore, learning to listen to God will help me in my listening to people and *vice versa*. Further, none of these areas are mutually exclusive: we may hear God speaking to us as we counsel an individual. This should be borne in mind as we consider each area.

The sort of listening that is being discussed in this booklet is largely that done by an individual. This is not to undermine the value of corporate listening, it is simply that there is not enough room in a small booklet to cover both. However, many of the lessons learned through individual listening will help our corporate listening.

2   The Problem of Inner Deafness

If I want to listen to someone, then I am effectively wanting to become more aware of them.

I have to become aware of who they are, what they look like, and what they are talking about. Through this sense of awareness I absorb into my system an impression of this personality with whom I converse. Awareness is a close relative to listening. Awareness of course involves the use of sight. But it is as we see and look that we may also listen. Thus, for example, we may look at nature and become aware of a communication. We *see* the moon and stars and *hear* a message about the majesty of God. Thus the psalm-writer can say:

> When I look at the heavens, the work of thy fingers
> the moon and stars which thou hast established.
> What is man that thou art mindful of him
> and the son of man that thou dost care for him?
> O Lord, our Lord, how majestic is thy name in all the earth!
>
> (Ps 8.3,4,9)

For the artist John Constable, 'nature in her humblest forms, in leaves, in grass, in hedgerow flowers, could yield to the perceptive mind the flash of vision.'[5] The poet is also aware of the beyond in nature. William Blake was able

> To see the World in a grain of sand
> And Heaven in a wild flower.[6]

But you do not have to be a psalm-writer, an artist, or a poet to be aware of nature. You simply have to be willing to pause, to look around and give yourself permission to spend time thinking about what is around you; you become *aware*. This is the beginning of careful listening. It is using our full sense of hearing. But there is the problem that it is under-used, and many 'have ears but hear not' (Ps 135.17). They have the faculties for hearing, for being aware, yet do not use them. This failure to hear I have termed 'inner deafness.' Listed below are five causes of this inner deafness.

Hyperactivity

It was during the age of the railway, when the idea of man moving at speed was becoming a reality, that Ruskin wrote:

> The really precious things are thought and sight, not pace...It does a man...if he be truly a man, no harm to go slow, for his glory is not at all in going, but in being.[7]

Unfortunately, those words were hurried past and today many people live a way of life that reveals our unhealthy obsession with doing things as fast as possible. The same sense of rush can very easily creep into the life of the church. A. W. Tozer comments:

> 'The accent on the church today,' says Leonard Ravenhill, the English evangelist, 'is not on devotion, but on commotion.' Religious extroversion has been carried to such an extreme in evangelical circles that hardly anyone has the desire, to say nothing of the courage, to question the soundness of it. Externalism has taken over. God now speaks by the wind and the earthquake only; the still small voice can be heard no more. The whole religious machine has become a noisemaker. The adolescent taste which loves the loud horn and the thundering exhaust has got into the activities of modern Christians. The old question, 'What is the chief end of man?' is now answered, 'To dash about the world and add to the din thereof.' And all this is done in the name of Him who did not strive nor cry, nor make his voice to be heard in the streets.[8]

To sit and *be* with someone or with God, or with the local paper, is not to waste time, but is to make the most constructive use of it. In the face of hyperactivity we have to 'study to be quiet.' As this becomes a priority, so we begin to feel more relaxed if we are being quiet with God, or if we are spending an hour in constructive listening to someone. We feel less of the urge to 'get on and do something.' For the church minister, there is often pressure to be seen doing something, even sometimes in order to justify his existence. But this pressure has to be resisted, else lives will be lived in such a sense of rush and activity that the quality of ministry suffers, and the still small voice goes unheard.

There is nothing intrinsically wrong in high activity; what is wrong is where there is no freedom to pause, and also where there is activity without receptivity. It appears from the gospels that Jesus had a full timetable, and yet he was never rushed; he always had time to be with someone in their need, and to hear the voices that cried for help.

Hardness of Heart

One of the commonest reasons in the Old Testament for failure to hear God's word was hardness of heart. A classic example is the Pharaoh who failed to hear God's word to release the people of Israel. Similarly, the people of Israel are often urged not to harden their hearts to God, as this will mean failure to hear the Lord's voice to them (for example Deut 30.17). We have a plea in Psalm 95:

> For he is our God, and we are the people of his pasture
> and the sheep of his hand.
> O that today you would hearken to his voice!
> Harden not your hearts, as at Meribah
> As on the day at Massah in the wilderness.

The heart for the Hebrew writer was the very centre of man's personal life, and if this was hardened then it was impossible for him to listen, as his life was cold towards God. When we love someone, then we will want to listen, to show concern, and because of this concern we will be all the more able to listen clearly. Similarly, as we learn to love the Shepherd, so we will grow to hear his voice (See John 10.1-5). But if we harden our hearts, as they did at Meribah and Massah, then we will fail to hear his word to us. There is this close connection between loving and listening.

If we are counselling someone our hearts have to be open to them—that is we need to be 'for' them, hoping for the best for them, even if it costs us something. Without this we will be turning our ears away from them because we will not want to carry any of their burdens.

If we are counselling someone, we need to b hoping the best for them, even if it costs us something

Lack of Humility

A certain humility is needed if we are going to listen to God or man. Jesus, when relating that parable of the soils and the sower's seed (Mt 13) calls for those who 'have ears' to hear. These people are of the true soil, the true *humus*. They are humble to receiving, to hearing something new. They have not got all the answers, can be 'put right' without offence, and can be enthused about a subject that they had hitherto rejected. Anthony Bloom, considering this humus, says:

> It is silent, inconspicuous, dark and yet it is always ready to receive any seed, ready to give it substance and life.[9]

Listening to God's word with this humility is rewarding, just as the receptive soil is rewarded with a harvest.. Humility is also needed when listening to people who are sharing their problems. If we are listening only in order to impose on that person our recommendations for their life, then we will be of little help to them. If we are truly to listen, then we are to 'hear them out'; we must hold back our pastoral inclinations to direct their life. Then, when they have been able to speak, without fear of being undermined or even burdened by advice, they will have been able successfully to express how they are feeling and will be open to receiving your word for them. The counsellor also has to know a humility that is prepared to admit that he cannot see a way through the problem. If the counsellor is prepared to admit that he cannot understand, or that he cannot see a way through the problem, the person being counselled will be reassured that this counsellor is genuine, and that he is not there to give unrealistic or 'pat' advice and answers. At least he can be sure that his counsellor is *with* him in this unknown—he is not alone.

Fear of Pain

There is a cost to effective listening. Some of the things we hear are tragic and this can be painful. Listening to God can also be painful because we may hear about his suffering and death, an experience which has led many into an agony of spirit. Listening to the community can also be a cause of inner pain and turmoil. It was Trevor Huddleston's listening to the cry of the black people in South Africa during his time in Johannesburg that led to much conflict and pain in his own life.[10] And yet this is surely the way of our Master who suffered for us, and if this is the case then we have to follow joyfully, knowing that the pain is not without his support and healing strength.

There is one further pain we may fear in the listening ministry. Some feel that they cannot listen to certain emotionally upset people because they have unresolved fears within themselves. For example often people are unable to listen and be with the bereaved because they are unable to face either their own death or the death of a loved one. They therefore refuse to listen and the person who is seeking a listener feels alone with an added sense of rejection. Dr. Frank Lake writes:

> If you are one of the rare people who does want to listen, you will have to make it plain, against the current trend, that you will not retaliate with the feared rejection, even if the sharing and the effect of the material shared is to take you into your own areas of mental pain.[11]

If these areas of mental pain do come to the surface during counselling, then there is clearly a need for them to be looked at and brought before the healing touch of God.

Failure to Listen to Self

Within each of us there are voices—guilt, despair, fear or longings. Some of these are expressed, others are repressed. If we keep ourselves constantly busy and 'protected,' then, unless there is some crisis, the repressed voices stay hidden. But though they are hidden, they have an influence on our behaviour. Naturally we are not inclined to listen easily to these. But nevertheless they are there, and if we fail to listen to them, we will not be able to hear clearly the inner voices of others, or of my community. Neither will we be able to hear the voice of God clearly if we are holding part of ourselves back from him. We will be listening only selectively. An obvious example is this: if I have grown up with and still live amongst excesses of wealth, there may be within me a voice of guilt whenever I meet poverty. If I have not faced up to this voice, then in order to avoid the voice of guilt, I will also avoid the cry of the poor. But if I start listening to the voices within I can assess whether the guilt is valid and ask questions about my own lifestyle. I am also free to listen without fear or prejudice to the voice of the poor.

Neither will we be able to hear the voice of God clearly if we are holding part of ourselves back from him

The best place to listen to our voices within is in the place of quiet before the Lord. Mother Mary Clare writes:

> We probably won't like what we hear, but once we have begun to be really still, and have stopped deluding ourselves with our own ideas and suggestions, there is a chance that we may hear within ourselves what we most deeply desire but may still be afraid to face.[12]

As I listen to the voices within myself I will hear the fears, the guilts and desires. These may be hard to face, and yet facing them will produce growth in my life. Under the care of the Father I pause and listen and grow. It is part of my maturing in Christ, and this helps me to become more of a listening sort of person.

Listening to God

3

It is vitally important that we learn to listen to God's communication to us.

This chapter explores the why, when and how of personal listening to God — though we must not forget the importance of the church's corporate listening to God too.

Why Listen to God

The Bible makes it clear that God is a God who desires to communicate with his creation. Psalm 29 speaks of the power of the voice of the Lord:

> The voice of the Lord is upon the waters;
>   the God of glory thunders,
>   the Lord, upon many waters.
> The voice of the Lord is powerful;
>   the voice of the Lord is full of majesty.   (Ps 29.3,4)

God desires to communicate with us. He hears the cry of the individual (Ps 94.9; 116.1), and he speaks to us. To listen to the Lord is the way to life, but failure to hear his voice brings disaster. Thus in Deuteronomy 1.43 and 44:

> So I spoke to you and you would not hearken; but you rebelled against the command of the Lord and were presumptuous and went up into the hill country. Then the Amorites who lived in that hill country came out against you and chased you as bees do and beat you down in Seir as far as Hormah.

The New Testament tells us that God still speaks to his people and that this time 'he has spoken by a Son' (Heb 1.2). At the transfiguration the word of God to the disciples about his Son is the command to 'Listen to him' (Mk 9.7). It is clear from Scripture that we should listen to the Lord. But what is the importance of listening to God?

The main reason is so that we can become more human. Our life is impoverished if we do not communicate with our Creator. People cannot live 'by bread alone'; they must also to be filled by 'every word that proceeds from the mouth of God' (Mt 4.4). We are created to respond to our Maker. and by doing this, to use Martin Buber's language, each person becomes 'I' as he or she communicates with 'Thou.' If God does not communicate with us, he is only an 'It'; if he speaks to us, and we speak with him, he becomes 'Thou.' And as he speaks to us, we find our true identity. When the Father spoke to his Son at the Transfiguration, he affirmed 'This is my beloved Son.' Jesus knew who he was in the sight of his Father. Dietrich Bonhoeffer agonized over his own identity during his confinement in the prison cell, but came to this profound realization:

> Who am I? They mock me, these lonely questions of mine.
> Whoever I am, thou knowest, O God, I am thine.[13]

Bonhoeffer knew that he was truly himself when he was aware of being in the care and protection of God. For this knowledge he had to listen to the Lord's voice assuring him of this truth.

Through listening to God, we find we are given a sense of value and of purpose. In the context of this, we may also listen to God for direction, exhortation and correction. We need the word of God for our lives, and it is to him that we bring all our fundamental experiences of life. We bring not only the positive experiences, but also the negative. It is particularly necessary to listen to God when we find ourselves in the dark places of longings, loneliness, fears, protests or anger. In such places we need the healing word of God. This is beautifully expressed by George Herbert in his poem *The Collar*, where he cries in anger and protests to heaven, and is suddenly brought to a place of peace by one simple word from God:

> But as I rav'd and grew more fierce and wilde
> At every word,
> Me thoughts I heard one calling, *Child:*
> And I reply'd, *My Lord.*[14]

George Herbert discovered that the result of listening to God's word was not only a sense of value and purpose, but also a sense of submission.

The Bible makes it clear that we serve a God who desires to communicate with his creation and that failure to listen to his word is not a light omission. God desires to speak to me, as his disciple; he desires to speak about himself, about me, and about the world and people to whom I minister. We all need to hear God speaking; we need to hear him speak about the sort of God he is. Especially we need to hear him speak to us of his love, as this profoundly affects our own nature. As Carretto writes,

> The love of God is by nature pure, balanced and holy. Whoever is dominated by it lives in deep peace, has an ordered view of things and knows the meaning of true freedom.[15]

As we listen to God speaking of his love for us, we change. As he speaks to us about ourselves we find direction for our lives. As he speaks to us about our ministry in his world, we find we are involved in fruitful work for the Kingdom of God. It is therefore crucial both for our sense of being and for our doing, that we clearly hear the voice of God.

When to Listen to God

There are of course no set times for listening to God. In any meaningful relationship between two people there is the freedom to speak, to listen or to be silent at any point during the day. Where this is not so the relationship is strained. A marriage could justifiably be considered unsatisfactory if the husband refused to listen to his wife except for half an hour in the morning and a few minutes in the evening. The same applies in a person's relationship with God; it is unsatisfactory if he is only expecting God to speak on one or two occasions during the day. However, whilst it is good to be readily receptive to God's voice at any point during the day, it is also necessary to give some time of the day to a specific preparing of oneself for listening to God. As we go on to consider how to listen to God, we shall be thinking particularly of this time set apart from the day's activities where there is the minimum chance of interruptions and a reasonable guarantee of peace and quiet.

In the ministry of Jesus, there are times when he chooses to be apart from the activities of life, to be alone with his Father.[16] He needed the stillness and the quiet and length of time, so that he could have a time of uninterrupted communication with his Father. There are two important ingredients for this time apart with the Father: quietness and solitude. Not everyone finds solitude easy, and yet to be alone from time to time is important and necessary for our welfare. In his very helpful book on prayer, J Neville Ward comments

> Mature human beings need to be alone, and wish to be alone, for some time almost every day. It is a wish for deliberately chosen solitude that is going to be used creatively.[17]

This is not, he points out, an enforced loneliness, brought about by circumstances, but an actual choosing to be apart from one's fellow creatures for a space of time during the day, in order to be quiet. Dietrich Bonhoeffer also mentions the need for solitude when he writes about community life:

> Let him who cannot be alone beware of community. He will only do harm to himself and to the community. Alone you stood before God when he called you; alone you had to answer that call; alone you had to struggle and pray; and alone you will die and give an account to God. You cannot escape from yourself.[18]

Bonhoeffer was someone who knew many hours of aloneness in the prison cell and, because he had in previous years learned the value of solitude, could make constructive use of such solitude. But there is a cost involved in going into your room and praying to your Father who is in secret. The cost is partly that the time may seem unproductive—you do not actually produce anything in such a time, and other things which demand attention will usually be rapping on the door when you are spending time in quiet. The difficulty is convincing those things that your listening time is a priority, and it *is* a priority, because time spent in this way will influence the day's work. Those who have spent time receiving God's word and peace are bound to have more to offer in their day's work. This time will also make them more open and receptive to what God is saying to them at other points during the day.

There is also another part to the cost of being alone, which is to do with the listening to self that we mentioned in the previous chapter. If we become quiet, then we are likely to start hearing the voices within ourselves that perhaps we try to drown by being in company with others. Bonhoeffer observed this:

> Many people seek fellowship because they are afraid to be alone. Because they cannot stand loneliness, they are driven to seek the company of other people. There are Christians, too, who cannot endure being alone who have some bad experiences with themselves, who hope they will gain some help in association with others.[19]

This time of silence therefore will require sometimes a facing up to fears, anxieties and the voices within that perhaps we have tried to avoid. In this time, in the company of the Lord all these voices have to be heard, not avoided. In the stillness we may well be aware of the voice of the living God speaking to our fears.

Sometimes it may be good to take an extended time of quiet away from home or work. A quiet day, or a retreat of several days away, can be most beneficial. Many convents and monasteries are only too pleased to cater for such needs.

How to Listen

Traditionally it has been the Catholic wing of the church that has found value in contemplative prayer and the use of silence. It has also been very much part of Eastern Orthodox spirituality. However, in recent years, other branches of the church, who for a long time viewed such activity with great suspicion, have been discovering the value of silence and contemplation. Naturally one wants to avoid the excesses and also to avoid confusion with such practices as transcendental meditation. One also wants to avoid escapism and unreality. However, there is a very clear and definite Christian tradition of quiet and contemplation which is most constructive, and to which, if we wish to grow in our listening to God, we would do well to refer.

The approach to how we listen to God will vary with each individual but there are some general guidelines which may be helpful.

(a) Silence

We have mentioned above the need for quiet when we find a time to listen to God. This is somewhere on our own. But we will find, even on our own, that though there may be exterior silence, there may not be interior silence. It is not easy to become inwardly quiet. The Russian poet, Yevtushenko, has written about silence:

> Insight is the child of silence.
> No matter if we make no tumult:
> We must calmly shed all noise
> In the name of the new leaves.[20]

To become inwardly silent requires us laying down for a moment all our plans, arrangements, burdens, all noise. The reward of this is insight—insight about God and ourselves.

(b) Relaxation and Posture

If we are to be quiet, we have to relax. Regular breathing and a comfortable posture for prayer help relaxation. The posture for prayer is important. It is difficult to be attentive to God (or to anyone) slouched in an armchair. God has given us bodies to help in our lives and they are an important feature in our communication system. Therefore when we pray and listen to God, we want not to deny the existence of our bodies, but to get them to join in our prayer.[21] In the diagrams we have three possible positions for listening and prayer. There are many others such as standing and prostration; but these are ones which many find helpful.

Figure 1 illustrates the usual kneeling position. This position speaks of humility before the Lord, and is useful in prayers of penitence and supplication. But you will find it is hard to keep up this position for any length of time!

Figure 2 is the standard seated position. Notice the straight back and the horizontal position of the thighs—this is the healthiest position for sitting and the most comfortable for a long time of quiet.

Figure 3 illustrates the use of the prayer stool which helps you to sustain a relaxed kneeling position. Whatever posture you adopt for your listening, it is wise to use it regularly so that it grows in naturalness and comfort.[22]

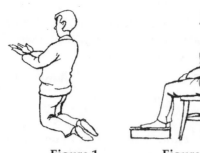

Figure 1	Figure 2	Figure 3

(c) Listening Aids

The primary aid to help us listen to the voice of God is of course the Bible. It is the essential channel of God's communication to use. There are also a number of secondary aids:

Devotional Books are often a means through which God speaks to us. But remember such books are at their best when read thoughtfully and slowly.

Visual Aids —a picture or a candle—can help in focussing attention.

Repetitious prayer such as the Jesus prayer is used by many to help them focus their minds on the Lord. For those whose minds quickly wander, this can be a helpful anchor.[23] Sentences of Scripture are also very helpful when repeated and meditated upon.

Songs and hymns As long as no neighbours are disturbed, sing to the Lord and enjoy it! Singing expresses our love and praise for God and also can bring quietness to our souls.

Speaking in tongues can be a most useful way in to quietness for those who have this gift.

When there is a corporate meeting such gifts as prophecy, used with discernment, will be an important means of listening to God's will.

These are just some aids to help you as you attempt to listen to God. Sometimes his word may be hard to hear or understand. Sometimes there may be long silences from heaven. At other times there may be the joy of a clear word from the Father. When the word is clear, it is always important to remember that the word comes to the *humus*, the humble soil. This quality of humility should house and protect the word, so that, should it be appropriate to share it, the hearers should experience not an arrogant announcement of an infallible 'The Lord has told me…' but a sense of the gratitude and grace with which the word was received. There also needs to be an openness to test and discern, that the whole body may be convinced that God has spoken.[24]

Listening to an Individual 4

The person who learns to listen to God learns to become more receptive to and aware of other areas of life, and this is particularly true when we come to consider listening to individuals.

In this chapter we shall be discussing the listening that is involved when we are with an individual who has come for counselling, but it should be noted that we learn to listen not just to become better counsellors, but to improve our relationships in general. One does not have to look far to see how often relationships turn sour, or simply never begin, because of poor listening. Listening to an individual is an activity that demands careful thought, consideration and learning.

Listening to an individual is an activity that demands careful thought, consideration and learning

If we are prepared to listen, and to grow in our listening work, then we become of great service to the ministry of the church. There are many who want to be listened to. All of us at some time or other want to be listened to. It is a fundamental human need. There are reasons for this desire; if I have someone who will listen to me, I immediately have a sounding-board. I can hear what it sounds like when I articulate my problem. This in itself can clarify the problem. Whatever the nature of this problem the risk is that I become more unattractive with it. Therefore if I can express it to someone who still accepts me with my problem, I feel more secure, more able to face the issues involved. I do not have to face the added burden of feeling alone or despised because of my pain. The bereaved person, for example, finds great relief in finding someone he can talk to who does not treat him as some freak or peculiar creature. Pain can often be very isolating. The great relief about being listened to is that the listener has given me sufficient value to think I am someone with whom it is worth spending time.

If we look to the ministry of Jesus we find in him someone who, in his dealings with individuals, showed a remarkable understanding and wisdom in the way he listened to them. It is worth doing a Bible study on Jesus' encounter with individuals to notice the way he would always listen to each one's particular need and then address that need. We have to learn, as effective listeners, to hear all that is being communicated. We do not communicate with our speech alone; we communicate with the whole message. Below are listed the important things we need to be listening to when we are with individuals.

What to Listen to

1 *Words*: Note carefully the use of words. What sort of words are being used? Are they 'thinking' words or 'feeling' words? Notice especially the use of strong feeling words such as 'hate,' 'crushed,' 'dark,' 'cannot stand.' How are the words being expressed? Where words are particularly emphasized or repeated is a sign that the person is touching on an important area.

2 *Silences*: If we are getting used to the idea of being silent with God, then we will not find it too difficult being silent with people. Do not hurry out of silences, or badger the person with questions each time she pauses. Give her room to think and feel. Much can happen in a silence—it is not awkward providing you are in control of it.

3 *Thinking*: As the individual is talking to you, what is going on in her thinking, in her understanding of things? If, for example, you are speaking with someone who is depressed through a strong sense of personal failure, can you notice in her thinking an attitude which says 'I am only acceptable to God and to others by coming up to a certain standard through doing good works'? Could she be helped by experiencing the truths within the theology of grace?

4 *Emotions*: Learning to listen to the emotions is crucial. The person who is talking to you may or may not be aware of what is going on in him emotionally. Your job is to help him understand and to handle his emotions if that is the need. Often there is the need to express tears, and if these want expressing then they should be expressed and not driven back by unrealistic words of comfort. The depressed person may have a real need to be tearful in your presence. It will be of great help to him if he can weep in safety with your simply being with him, without being rebuked by simplistic comments that all will be all right in the end. The body needs to express feelings, and the good listener will allow the expression of such feelings and will also be listening to what sort of anguish is being expressed.

5   *Facial expression*: What are the person's eyes doing as she talks to you? Can they look at you? At what points do they find it hard to look at you? When does the person smile or frown—and does it conflict with what she is saying? We are all familiar with the person who says with a frown on her face how much she loves her mother-in-law. The frown may betray how she honestly feels!

6   *Body Language*: What is the body saying while the person is talking? His posture may be speaking about how he is really feeling. He may find it very difficult to articulate verbally how he is, but the drooping head and slumped body will be speaking of some sort of depression. Look out also for times when hands start fidgeting or breathing becomes strained for sighs, nervous cough and so forth. These may all be part of the body trying to communicate areas of pain and difficulty.

It is important for us as listeners to learn with compassion how to read the complete language of the person and where it seems helpful to check out with him what we are hearing. We are not trying to catch him out or to play psychological games with him—we are simply trying to listen to the whole person.

Having discussed what we need to be listening to, I now draw attention to some aids that will help us to listen helpfully and effectively. Many of these are obvious, but we include them anyway as it is only too easy to overlook the obvious. The following aids apply to situations where you are giving individuals a substantial length of time and where they have specifically asked to see you about their problem.

Aids to Effective Listening

1. Show that you are listening with appropriate nods and affirmative words. Keep looking at the person and do not start yawning or looking out of the window! It is very important for the person to feel that you are giving him your full attention, and that you are not thinking about your next engagement. Good listening will give time and full attention to the person. Poor listening will be conveyed by fidgeting, finger drumming, rapid speech, watch-glancing, hostile stare and so on. Avoid these!

2. Be quiet within yourself. Pray beforehand for stillness, and for the peace of Christ to be resting in your heart. Make sure you are in a reasonably quiet place where you do not have to strain to hear the person, and try to eliminate possible distractions.

3. Make sure that the room is comfortable and check practical arrangements such as warmth, comfort, tea. Do not sit in front of a bright light or a window, as the person will only see you in silhouette, which is disconcerting. Have a box of tissues handy when there is the likelihood of tears.

4. Be genuine. A listener who is pretending to be someone she is not is generally unhelpful. The person will pick up what is genuine, and will be made to feel unsure by what is false. Genuineness in the listener will produce genuineness in the person being listened to.

5. Remember that listening is a non-directive exercise. Later you may want to give direction, but while you are listening, you are gaining information and helping the person to see where she is. You are not primarily giving advice or solving problems. The person wants to be sure she is heard before she is able to receive direction. The very act of your listening may, of course, help her to clarify her thoughts, and enable her to find for herself the direction she needs.

6. Show empathy. It is important to distinguish empathy from sympathy. We are all familiar with sympathy, the showing of feelings of compassion. Empathy is well described in Harper Lee's novel *To Kill a Mockingbird*, where Atticus is sharing some of his wisdom with his daughter, Scout:

> 'First of all, he said, 'if you can learn a simple trick, Scout, you'll get along a lot better with all kinds of folks. You never really understand a person until you consider things from his point of view —'
>
> 'Sir?'
>
> '—until you climb into his skin and walk around in it.'[25]

An empathetic response shows a willingness to understand the person's attitude and feelings without judging him for it. You can understand the feelings, and yet still stay emotionally detached. You are not becoming emotionally part of the person's experience (sympathy). You are not just feeling sorry for the person, but you are making a real attempt to 'climb into his skin' and understand why the person is responding and feeling as he is. Sympathy does of course have a therapeutic value in counselling, but empathy allows you to maintain an objective view of the situation.

7. Be prepared to suspend judgment. If someone comes and confesses something which she knows to be wrong, do not show shock or immediate censorship. She is sharing with you because she trusts you not to reject her. To judge her leaves her in isolation, and enforces further guilt, whereas to show understanding helps to lead her through. Failure to judge does not imply a condoning of the wrong, simply an understanding that we have all sinned and we all need God's forgiveness and healing. Be sure to respect the person and to reflect the attitude 'you are free to be exactly who you are without risk or blame. You are free to be you, not my expectations of you.'

8. Be aware of important relationships. Listen to the family needs and demands. Which relationships are satisfactory, and which have indications of pain and stress, either in the present or in the past?

9. It may help you to take a few notes. Check this with the person first.

10. Be aware of the 'here and now' situation. What is going on in the person as he talks? What is going on in you as you listen? What is going on between you?

11. Where it seems appropriate, confront the person and challenge him about what he is saying. There may be discrepancies between what he is communicating verbally and through body language. Confrontation has to be sensitively handled in order to maintain trust.

12. Try to get away from rambling stories; focus on specific events and feelings.

13. Use the person's own language. Reflect back some of the words that she uses.

14. Be silently in prayer when possible, and where appropriate, pray together. Be open to the workings of the Holy Spirit who may, through a word of knowledge or prophetic insight reveal to you an important area of this person's life that is causing trouble, of which neither of you would otherwise be aware.[26]

15. Where the person has been made aware of sin in his life, lead him to a place where he can be assured of his absolution. The word of absolution from a priest can be extremely meaningful for those who are familiar with the tradition.[27] Be aware of any influences of evil that may be hindering the person's life. Ministry to this area is complex and dangerous and obviously needs much skill and care.[28]

16. Make sure at the beginning that you are clear about the time you are going to spend together. This gives the person a security and you the freedom to end the session at a definite time. If the person knows the time is limited, the quality of the time can often be improved.

The above notes are not a recipe for success, but are simply aids to help in the listening work. It may be useful after a counselling time to look back over these notes, and with their help, to observe how deeply you listened.

5 Listening to Society

I find that autumn helps me to listen to society.

This is for a purely practical reason. From where I sit at my desk in my study, I can look up and see the trees at the end of the garden. In the summer I enjoy their greenery and shade, but come the autumn, the curtain of leaves are taken away and I can look through the bare branches and look on a section of the parish in which I live. Now, as I see this part of the parish, and become aware of it, I begin to hear some voices. I can hear from the old peoples' home a cry of loneliness, a cry of anger and frustration at a growing deafness, and a cry of grief at the death of a beloved wife. I can hear from the council flats cries of despair from single mothers, wounded and bored. I can hear people as they battle with cold winds to get to the shops, resigning themselves to thinking that life is only to do with the material. I can also hear the unemployed, the vandal, the powerless, the lost. I am also aware of voices of joy, but somehow it is the needs which seem so prominent, and there are many other voices that I do not hear because of my own areas of inner deafness. As I listen to these voices, I also become aware that the voices are not just coming from outside my study, but they are also from in here. I, took, am a human being. I, too, like the others, have needs. But for me there is a difference.

I have a responsibility to serve the people amongst whom I live, as salt serves the earth and light the world

The majority of the people to whom I am listening do not have a meaningful relationship with God. I, by grace, have. This does not make me superior, but it does have two important consequences. Firstly, it means that I will know something of God's feelings about the cries of human need that he hears. Secondly, as a disciple of Jesus Christ, I have a responsibility to serve the people amongst whom I live, as salt serves the earth and light the world (Mt 5.13-16). I, and those who form the church in this area, have a positive contribution to make to the society in which we

We have to learn to practise what Carlo Carretto calls 'contemplation in the streets'

find ourselves. But before we can speak or act, we must listen. We have to learn to practise what Carlo Carretto calls 'contemplation in the streets,' which is, as he points out, 'a good phrase, but very demanding.'[29] Carretto is one of the Little Brothers of Jesus who feel called to live their religious life not in the cloister, but in the street. He writes of this call:

> You must go back among men, mix with them, live your intimacy with God in the noise of their cities. It will be difficult, but you must do it. And for this the grace of God will be with you.[30]

This is the call for those who are to be as salt and light. To listen to society, we must be part of it, exposing ourselves to the cries. Then we can begin to respond to the needs. But the listening work is not complete, for if we start responding when we have only heard the cries of society, then we will find ourselves in a frantic activity of visiting, counselling, campaigning, the needs always knocking at our door telling us to do something else. Our ministry to these needs has to begin with our 'intimacy with God.' Cardinal Suenens puts it like this:

> The Christian's involvement in the temporal and historical is more than a duty prescribed by the world's urgent needs and sufferings. It is an integral part of his relation to God, of the God-centred and eschatological aim of his faith and prayer.[31]

Our involvement in society therefore needs not only a listening to society, but a listening to God also. If we listen *only* to society, and try to respond to the cries we hear, without listening to God, then we shall find ourselves involved in inappropriate or even counter-productive ministry. By listening to God, we discern the priorities, and discover to which areas God is calling us to minister. So, as I sit at my study window, listening to the cries, I have also to be receptive to God, to hear his direction and to receive the Holy Spirit for the tasks to which he calls me.

I want now to discuss three important areas of Christian activity to illustrate how a prior listening to society can help our ministry. The three areas I have chosen are those of *Caring, Faith-sharing* and *Proclamation*.

Listening and Caring

The ways in which the church cares for the society around it will be multifarious. The minister will be involved in visiting the needy, ministering to the sick, comforting the bereaved, burying the dead. His ministry will extend far beyond his own flock out into the world. Hopefully in many of his tasks which take him out into his parish, he will be joined by members of his church. He is enabling his church to be salt and light in the local community.

As we begin to listen, we first have to deal with the sort of inner deafness that we discussed earlier. Most of us will be deaf to certain cries from society, and it is important to identify where a particular area of deafness might be. As you look out over society there will be some things that you do not want to see, or that you dismiss quickly. For example, take a moment to listen to the young people of your parish. What are they saying? What is the cry of their heart today? How are they expressing themselves? As you listen to the type of music they enjoy, can you hear something of what they might be trying to say? Or (and this is where we meet the problem of inner deafness) have you dismissed such music as 'rubbish' or even as 'of the devil'? We all have our area of prejudices, and most older people do not consider paying much attention to the sort of music that is so important to the young person.

It is all too easy to judge from a sense of fear or threat, and we thus become deaf

If a large area of a person's life is dismissed as 'rubbish,' then he will not find it easy to receive advice or direction from those who have not bothered to listen to him and his sphere of interests. It is common for people to judge before they have given a fair hearing. Yet Jesus said, 'As I hear, I judge, and my judgment is just, because I seek not my own will, but the will of him who sent me' (Jn 5.30). Jesus listened before he judged. He listened carefully to what was being said, and then listened to his Father's opinion. Then he was in the position of making an unbiased judgment in accordance with the will of the one who sent him. It is all too easy to judge from a sense of fear or threat, and we thus become deaf. If we are to be salt and light, then we must be healed from our inner deafness and risk listening, even if it hurts us.

Those who enjoy Chopin or Mozart may find it very difficult listening to contemporary songs on Top of the Pops, and yet if we are to hear what young people are trying to say, these must be listened to. It is easy to judge the modern music scene, but much harder to listen, and to listen deeply, to the cries within this music. Remember, listen not only to the words, but also to the type of music, the way it is presented, the clothes and expressions of the artists etc. Listen to the whole message. What do you hear? From time to time you will hear perhaps some of the deepest cries of our young people. For example, when I was running a youth group in the 1980's, I encouraged them to listen carefully to the words of pop songs. One favourite at the time was by 'The Police' called 'So lonely' which included this line:

> In this desert that I call my soul
> I always play the starring role.

If we have ears to hear, then it is not difficult to hear the cry in this, and how rich the gospel is, to speak to this desert.

You may like to go on to think about listening to such things as football hooliganism, vandalism, discontent in industry, family breakdown, racial problems. How can you gear your church to be effective at listening to needs for care in your area? What other groups are trying to listen? Are you in touch with them?

Listening and Faith Sharing[32]

It is clear from the New Testament that the disciples of Christ are expected to share their faith with others. Only some will be gifted evangelists (Eph 4.11), but all are part of a faith which is relevant to all people, and therefore can be shared. The church is made up of those who are 'ransomed, healed, restored, forgiven,' and this is the sort of good news that others want to hear about. The church therefore has a responsibility to tell others of this news. How faith-sharing is 'done' varies greatly, and there are many aids, techniques, tracts and teaching manuals that are published today to help us in this task. However, if these aids are used without a prior listening to the person with whom the gospel is being shared, then it is possible for more harm to be done than good.

By listening to the person with whom we are sharing our faith, we are showing a respect for them. We are saying: 'You have a value to me, not as an object for conversion, but as *yourself*. Because you mean a lot to me, I want you to have life in all its fullness, which is to be found in Christ.' Such a respect comes from our own experience of grace. It was the Japanese evangelist, Masumi Toyatome, who coined the phrase, 'the evangelistic ear.'[33] He talks of the crucial importance of deeply listening to the person's need, when we come to sharing our faith with them. If we listen carefully to the person's needs, then we can bring the good news of Jesus to that place of need. If we fail to do this, our message can appear irrelevant and even, at times, offensive.

If we listen to a person's needs, then we can bring the good news of Jesus to that place of need

For example, suppose Mary wants to share the gospel with her neighbour, Jean. Summoning up courage, she goes round to Jean one day and speaks to her about her need for repentance and the steps she can take to come to Christ. For some people this approach might have been helpful, but for Jean it is an unhappy experience. Jean is still in darkness after the death of her son in a motor accident, and she has been struggling with depression and severe grief. As far as she is concerned, God has treated her cruelly, and Mary is part of his conspiracy. Of course, the message that Mary is bringing is deeply relevant to Jean's needs, but Jean needs evidence that Mary is *really* concerned for her, if she is to believe that

25

she is genuine, and that her message is true. If Mary had taken the time to listen to the deep cries from Jean's heart, she would have been able to select those parts of the gospel that were relevant to Jean's needs. In this way she would have communicated God's care and love for Jean, and also his word to her.

A man dying of starvation needs to be given some bread as well as the gospel, otherwise the gospel will have no integrity. We find that Jesus always carefully listened to the people to whom he ministered. We looked earlier at the incident of his meeting with the Samaritan woman and saw how Jesus listened to her deepest needs, and by accurately hearing these, he was able to bring the gospel right to her point of need. A sensitive listening will greatly help the effectiveness of our faith-sharing, and will earn us the right to speak.

Listening and Proclamation

In its role as light to the world, the church is required to speak out, to proclaim on the housetops what it has heard whispered in secret (Mt 10.27). God desires to speak to his creation through his people. In the Old Testament, it was the prophets who were to speak out the word of God, not only to Israel, but to Babylon, Egypt, Moab and other foreign powers. The Lord warns his creation, and speaks before he acts. Thus Amos writes:

> Surely the Lord does nothing without revealing his secret to his servants the prophets. (Amos 3.7)

The prophet proclaimed God's word in the power of the Spirit. After the gift of the Spirit at Pentecost, there is no longer this restriction to just one or two prophets, but now many are able to proclaim God's word. One of the first results of the gift of the Spirit at Pentecost is Peter's proclamation to the crowds gathered outside the upper room. He spoke of God's plan for these people.

The church has a duty to proclaim God's plan to society. There has to be the general proclamation of 'repent and be baptized.' The church is there to speak to society about God's desire for men, women and children to come to repentance and life. But how much does this really go on? How often does society hear the word of God? How often does the secular man hear the word of God concerning spiritual or social issues? The church is responsible for proclaiming to the world the mind of God. David Pawson says:

> Christians have got to tell Britain how God feels. I believe this nation is waiting for someone to tell it how God feels—e.g. that he is sick of things like lukewarm churches, of Christmas celebrations by people who have no intention of knowing him; of abortions which throw a

baby away every five minutes. Or that he is glad of a few things in Britain today—that two out of three marriages stay together; that children do not run around today with polio and rickets.

The Old Testament prophets told Israel how God felt. We have got to do that. It makes us and the nation aware of God, that he is a living God, and that this world is his.[34]

David Pawson is talking about our responsibility to our nation. It needs to hear the mind and heart of God. But the proclamation is not just national; it is also local. What is God saying to the people beyond my garden fence? What injustice does he want to speak against? What goodness does he want to encourage?

To be messengers of God's word in the world is not an easy task. It is one which is not happening as much as it should. This is partly because we are poor listeners. We have not heard those cries, those questions to heaven that need a reply. The cries can only be heard as we are *in* the world, listening.

But also there is a great need to be in our place of quiet, listening to the whisper of God that must be proclaimed from the housetop. We have to listen for his word which he wants us to proclaim to society, whether it is just over the fence, or nationally.

We have not heard those cries, those questions to heaven that need a reply

I, personally, am aware of being very much a beginner in this listening work, but I believe it is a crucial area in the ministry of the church to the world. Perhaps we can (individually and in groups) do further thinking on this area to work out how we can learn to listen to God for his world, and to learn how and through what means his word can be best communicated. When we have had the humility and the wisdom to listen, then we shall have the authority and the knowledge with which to speak.

Notes

1   O W Holmes, 'The Poet at the Breakfast Table' Chapter 10 quoted in the *Oxford Dictionary of Quotations* (Second Edition) 251.22.
2   Job's comforters did show wisdom at first by sitting silently with him in his suffering for seven days and nights (Job 2.13). However, when they began to speak it was more as an explanation of suffering based on their own theological presuppositions rather than as a response to an accurate listening to Job's predicament. Because of this, though Job feels he has been spoken to, he does not feel that he has been heard. Hence Job 31.35.
3   S Verney, *Into The New Age* (Fount Paperbacks, 1977) p 23.

4   Mother Mary Clare SLG, *Listening to God and Listening to Community* (Fairacres Publication 69, 1978) p 4.
5   C Peacock, *John Constable,The Man and His Work* (John Baker, 1965) p 44.
6   W Blake, 'Auguries of Innocence' in J Hayward (ed) *Penguin Book of English Verse* (1956) p 243.
7   Ruskin, *Modern Painters* (in *Works* V.380-1).
8   A W Tozer, *The Root of the Righteous* (USA: Christian Publications Inc, Second Asian Edition, 1972) p 661-2.
9   A Bloom, *Living Prayer* (DLT, 1972) p 98.
10 See T Huddleston, *Naught for your Comfort* (Fontana, 1957).
11 F Lake in a piece entitled *Listening and Responding* (CTA, First Year Syllabus) p 5.
12 Mother Mary Clare, *Listening to God* p 11.
13 D Bonhoeffer *Letters and Papers from Prison* (SCM enlarged edition, 1973) p 347f.
14 G Herbert's poem 'The Collar' in C A Patrides (ed) *The English Poems of George Herbert* (Dent, 1974) p 161f.
15 C Carretto, *Letters from the Desert* (DLT, 1978) p 29.
16 See Mk 1.35 where Jesus goes out to a lonely place. In this instance he goes 'a great while before day.' Whilst the early morning is an obvious time for this time of quietness, it is by no means the only possibility.
17 J Neville Ward, *The Use of Praying* (Epworth, 1970) p 127.
18 D Bonhoeffer, *Life Together* (SCM, 1972) p 57.
19 D Bonhoeffer, *Life Together* p 57.
20 Y Yevtushenko, 'Autumn' in D Weissbort (ed) *Post War Russian Poetry* (Penguin, 1974) p 159.
21 Some people find it easier to express to God what they are feeling through their bodies than through their words. Thus rather than verbalising a prayer, they may dance it, or say it through movements. This can be a very effective means of expression.
22 One of the dangers in advocating meditation and contemplation is that there are many books and teachers and courses that now encourage various eastern forms of meditation as useful aids in Christian prayer. It is important that we realize the underlying religious philosophy behind all of these practices because basically the Indian approach to prayer is radically different from the Christian way. Christian prayer always centres upon the person of God as revealed in Christ Jesus, whereas the Indian view encourages us to seek for the God who is within, indeed who is part of us, because Hindu thought in general sees no distinction between us and God—all reality is one. The Christian aim in prayer is so to become united in love and fellowship with God, the Father of our Lord Jesus Christ, that our whole life, body, soul and spirit discover that wholeness and unity which God intends for us as we become more like Christ. On the other hand, so many Indian techniques encourage a kind of spiritual trip outside of our bodies, which are seen as one of the main hindrances to transcendental meditation. Christian prayer seeks to deal with the problem of the body by bringing a true unity within the person; Indian ways solve the same problem by trying to escape from the body. John Richards has written a very useful article on 'Christians and Yoga' in *Renewal* No 68, April/May 1977 p 25.
23 See R M French, *The Way of a Pilgrim* (SPCK 1972) for an account of the use of this prayer. The prayer is simply 'Lord Jesus Christ, Son of the Living God, have mercy on me, a sinner,' which can be used in this complete form or in shorter versions.
24 For further helpful reading on this subject see p 24.
25 H Lee, *To Kill a Mockingbird* (Pan, 1974) p 35.
26 See the discussion of John 4 on pages 4-5 where Jesus exercises this prophetic insight.
27 For a helpful book on this subject of forgiveness, absolution and healing see M Scanlon, *The Power in Penance* (Ave Maria Press, 1972).
28 One of the most helpful books on the pastoral care of those involved with evil and the demonic is J Richards, *But Deliver Us From Evil* (The Seabury Press, 1974).
29 C Carretto, *Letters from the Desert* p 75.
30 C Carretto, *Letters* p 74.
31 Cardinal Suenens and Dom Helda Camara, *Charismatic Renewal and Social Action: A dialogue* (DLT, 1980) p 35.
32 I have called this section 'Faith Sharing' rather than 'Evangelism' to make a distinction. By 'Faith Sharing,' I am referring to the day-to-day sharing of our faith with non-believers; 'Evangelism' can speak of something more structured and involving those who have the gifts of evangelism.
33 He uses the term in notes that he produced on evangelism, published by Missionary Strategy Agency, Los Angeles in 1974.
34 D Pawson in *Buzz* (July 1980) p 48.